Reaching for the Sun

Kids in Cuba

Trish Marx
Photographs by Cindy Karp

The Millbrook Press

Brookfield, Connecticut

For Patrick — T.M.   *For my brother Steven — C.K.*

Many thanks to:
The William W. O'Neill Foundation, Jorge Gonzalez and the Cuban
Ministry of Culture, Judy Cantor, and, of course, Jonathan Kozol

— Trish Marx and Cindy Karp

Published by The Millbrook Press, Inc.
2 Old New Milford Road
Brookfield, CT 06804

Library of Congress Cataloging-in-Publication Data
Marx, Trish.
Reaching for the sun : kids in Cuba / Trish Marx ; photographs by Cindy Karp.
p. cm.
Summary: Details the experiences of a group of children from a Los Angeles creative arts organization who traveled
to Cuba to write and perform a play with a Cuban children's theater group in the summer of 2000.
ISBN 0-7613-2261-2 (lib. bdg.)
1. Children—Cuba—Social life and customs—20th century—Juvenile literature.
2. Cuba—Social life and customs—20th century—Juvenile literature.
3. Cuba—Social conditions—20th century—Juvenile literature.
4. SOL Project—Juvenile literature. [1. Cuba—Social life and customs. 2. Theater.
3. Culture. 4. Interpersonal relations. 5. SOL Project.] I. Karp, Cindy, ill. II. Title.
CURR F1760 .M36 2003
972.9106—dc21   2002012030

What Happened Before

Cuba is an island country 90 miles (145 kilometers) off the coast of Florida. For hundreds of years, it was home to the Arawaks, the Tainos, and other Indian tribes.

On his first voyage in search of the New World, Christopher Columbus landed on Cuban shores. Waves of explorers came after Columbus, searching for gold and other riches. They enslaved the native people. They also brought with them germs and weapons. When they left, most of the native people were dead of disease, famine, or war.

Over the years, the island was resettled by Spaniards, by natives who came from surrounding islands, and by Africans brought to Cuba to work as slaves on the large sugar, cotton, and tobacco plantations.

In 1868 a plantation owner named Carlos Manuel de Céspedes freed his slaves and asked other landowners to do the same. Many of the former slaves fought in an uprising against Spain. This small war may have been lost to history, except for one thing: Cubans say that the date of the uprising—October 10, 1868—is the day that defined who Cubans really are. They are not Spanish people, or African people, or people from the surrounding islands. On this day they became the Cuban people.

It took another thirty years before Spain's rule over Cuba ended, with the Spanish-American War. After that, Cuba was a republic with a constitution and elected officials, but also with widespread poverty and corruption in the government.

In 1959 a revolution led by Fidel Castro once again changed the government. After the revolution, Cuba and the United States, because they believed in different types of government, were no longer friendly toward each other. The United States imposed an embargo, which meant they would not trade with Cuba. They also made it against the law for people from the United States to travel to Cuba, unless they had special permission.

Even ideas were not allowed to flow between Cuba and the United States. People from the two countries didn't have a chance to know each other, so they didn't trust each other.

The next decades were very difficult for Cubans. The embargo created shortages. It was difficult for people to get things such as telephones, cars, and even food. What few resources they had, however, supported a school system that reached most of the population and a medical system that was one of the best in the Americas.

By the 1990s, while it was not easy for people from the United States to travel to Cuba, tourists from other countries went to enjoy Cuba's beautiful beaches, warm weather, and friendly people. Americans, too, were curious about their close neighbor. What if a group of children from the United States could do something that had not been done before? What if they could get special permission to travel to Cuba to live and work with Cuban children?

In the summer of 2000, a children's theater group from Cuba—La Colmenita, or Little Beehive—invited a children's creative arts organization from Los Angeles, Equal Opportunities Productions (EqOp), to Cuba. They would work together to write a play that would be performed at the National Theater of Cuba. Twelve mentors from each country were invited to work with them. (A mentor is like a counselor and a teacher and a friend all in one.) The entire group was called the SOL Project.

This is the story of what happened to one girl from Los Angeles, Angie Espinoza, age ten, during the month she lived and worked in Cuba.

Angie stepped off the plane. Cuba, at last! It was hotter than she had expected. People were speaking Spanish, a language that Angie spoke at home with her Mexican-born parents. Angie looked for her friends in the theater group she was traveling with from Los Angeles. They were boarding a bus that would take them to a children's camp in Parque Lenin, a large park on the outskirts of Havana, where they would spend the first night. There

the kids from La Colmenita were waiting. La Colmenita, or Little Beehive, was a Cuban children's theater group. Angie had been waiting weeks for this day, but now that it was here, she couldn't imagine how these two groups would be able to write and perform a play in just one month.

When they reached the park, Angie saw lush trees, flowering bushes, and green lawns surrounding low concrete buildings. Outside one building, twelve Cuban kids stood in a group, looking just as curious about the kids from Los Angeles as Angie was about them.

"*Hola,* my name is Evelin." Angie had just stepped off the bus. She looked up and saw a pretty, light-haired girl.

"I'm Angie," she said.

Evelin helped Angie carry her things. By the time they reached the room where the girls would sleep, they were chatting and giggling. The next morning, Angie and Evelin ran to the bus first so they could sit together on the long ride to Cienfuegos, where they were going to spend the next two weeks.

Cienfuegos, a town near the southwest coast of Cuba, is close to both the ocean and

the mountains. There the kids would write the play that they would put on at the National Theater of Cuba in Havana. But before they could work together, they needed to get to know each other.

Every day in Cienfuegos, the mentors led discussion groups for the kids to compare ideas and share stories about where and how they lived. Once they played a game about what the American and Cuban kids knew about each other's country. "I know that the United States is a democracy, and that Abraham Lincoln was an important president," said Ray, Evelin's brother.

Angie said before the trip she had gone to the library to get a book about Cuba. "I found only one," she said, "and I didn't know

anyone who had been to Cuba. It made me more curious to come."

The kids talked about their dreams and what they wanted to be when they grew up. "A doctor, because they help people," a Cuban boy said. "An actress or a lawyer, because they make money," answered a girl from Los Angeles. But they all said that if they worked hard enough, they could grow up to be whatever they wanted.

After a few days, the mentors suggested a theme for the play. They asked the kids to think about a baseball game. What if someone hit the ball so hard that it flew high into the air and got lost? What if the kids started looking for it, and their search took them through cities, into jungles, even far out to sea? And what if they did not find the ball? Would the journey be a failure? Or would they have become such good friends that it wouldn't matter?

A mentor asked them to think about something they would hate to lose.

"My Beanie Babies," said Angie.

"The doll I had when I was little," said Evelin.

But they agreed it would be much worse if they lost their friends.

In the end, the kids decided it was the journey that mattered, not what was lost. By going on a journey together, kids would get to know and understand each other. This is what was really important.

Because Angie spoke Spanish, she and Evelin could tell each other about their friends, and what they liked to do together. Later, they were able to talk about how scary it can be making a new friend and being away from their families. That little ache in Angie's stomach that told her she was homesick disappeared when she was with Evelin.

The kids worked together for two weeks in Cienfuegos. To help write the play, the mentors took the kids on field trips. For the scenes set on a mountain, they went to the mountains. For the scenes about water, they wrote by the sea. If they wrote about a forest, they found a grove of trees to sit in.

When they had a rough outline of the

play, they had to rewrite it. This meant they had to listen even harder to each other. What kind of music should they use for the city scene—salsa or rap? What kind of food should they miss while they are on their journey—hot fudge sundaes or tamales? They learned to compromise. They agreed to do the monologues in both Spanish and English. They started trusting and respecting each other's opinions.

By the time they left Cienfuegos, the EqOp and La Colmenita kids were like brothers and sisters. This is what the mentors had hoped would happen when they started The Sol Project.

Now the real work was about to begin!

Havana

For the next two weeks, the group stayed at Parque Lenin. Built for Cuban kids as a place where they could spend time studying dance,

gymnastics, painting, or exploring other things they were interested in, the Parque had large sunny spaces for rehearsing the songs, dances, and scenes from the play.

On the first day back in Havana, the kids and mentors piled into buses. They were going on a tour of the city.

Angie stared out the bus window. The streets were lined with big houses. Many had balconies and pillars and wrought-iron doors that opened to hallways with marble floors. Some of the houses were surrounded by strips of grass fenced in by flowering bushes and old ornate gates. Others were row houses, each painted a different fading color.

Angie could imagine the houses as they once looked. Now most needed work of some kind—a balcony had no railing, a front stoop was crumbling, a window or door was missing. Some houses had been repaired and painted in soft pinks and yellows and greens, but most stood like proud old soldiers patiently waiting for a new suit of armor.

On the streets, people rode bikes or drove the kinds of cars Angie saw only in old movies in the United States. Evelin told her that paint for the houses and gasoline for cars was expensive because they had to be bought from other countries and shipped to Cuba.

The kids hopped off the bus at a large white mansion with a huge tank in front. It was the Museum of the Revolution. More than forty years ago, Fidel Castro led an army of civilians against a government that many people thought was corrupt. The revolution lasted a little more than a year. When it was over, Cuba became a socialist country and Fidel Castro was its leader. Thousands of Cubans who were afraid of living under the new government fled the country. The people who stayed had to work hard to provide food, fuel, medicine, soap, shoes, and all the other things it takes to run a country with more than ten million people.

The next place the kids visited was a large building with a big dome. "It looks just like our Capitol building," said Angie. A Cuban mentor told her that the same person had designed both the U.S. Capitol, and this building, which was Cuba's former capitol. After the revolution, it was turned into offices and a science museum.

As they walked through Havana the kids saw women selling

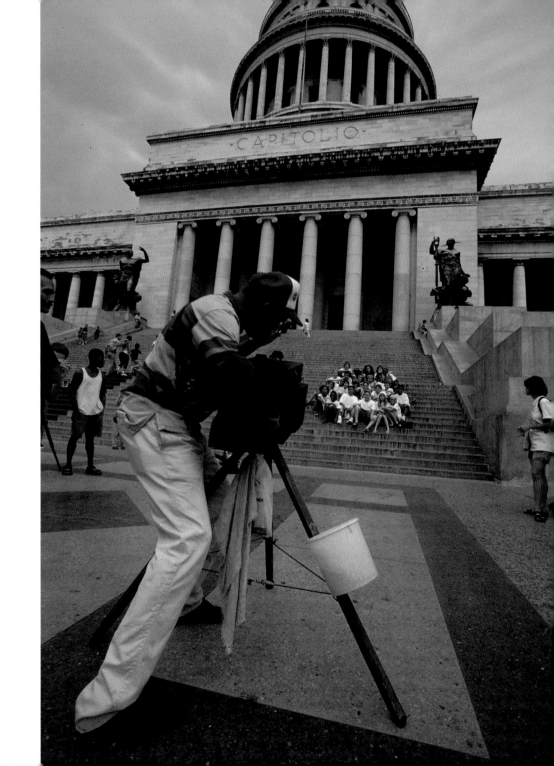

homemade lollipops. Further down the street was a small amusement park for young children, and street performers passing their

hats for contributions. They saw a market where Cubans can sell homegrown produce and flowers. "My mom's friends sometimes give us what they grow," Evelin told Angie. There is a Cuban saying that goes, "It is better to have a friend in Cuba than money."

Cubans rely on their friends for many things—trading houses, borrowing cars, lending wedding gowns, sharing newly slaughtered chickens raised in a friend's yard. Costumes for La Colmenita plays are often made from old dresses that people have saved. Sometimes the kids knock on neighborhood doors asking if there are any clothes, or even lipsticks and eye pencils, for La Colmenita.

Just when Angie thought she could not look at another sight, the buses stopped in front of a fast-food restaurant. It reminded Angie of McDonald's. Evelin said it was a treat to go there, because Cuban children don't often go out to eat.

They returned to Parque Lenin full and ready to work.

rice and beans. Foods such as mangoes and papayas are seasonal, so they are eaten only at certain times of the year. When Angie asked about apples, her Cuban friends shrugged their shoulders. Some of them had never eaten an apple, because apples do not grow naturally in Cuba.

Every day at the camp, after breakfast and again in the afternoon and evening, the children worked together on the play. They had to memorize their lines and practice them again and again.

"Time for a break," Michael, the director from Los Angeles, said. "There is ice cream for everyone at the snack stand." When they came back, they were ready to concentrate again.

"Edgar, your turn," said Michael.

Practicing and Playing

The next day at breakfast time, Angie and Evelin linked arms and walked to the dining hall. A plate of mangoes sat next to cereal, eggs, sausage, and rice and beans. The children could also choose oranges, papaya, star fruit, and bananas. Almost every meal in Cuba includes

Edgar's voice reached across the room where Gabe, a mentor from Los Angeles, was sitting. "When I think of joy, I think of cool, cool Kool-Aid kids on a sunny, Sunday afternoon. . . ."

"Louder," yelled Gabe. "The theater will be filled with people." And Edgar said his lines louder, until Gabe was satisfied.

Other times they worked on the dance routines. First they watched a Cuban dance mentor, and then they lined up behind him, stepping and turning until they could do it without looking.

One scene called for jugglers. Jake, a mentor from Los Angeles, counted 1 – 2 – 3 over and over as he and the children threw beanbags up in the air. At first, more beanbags fell on the ground than stayed in the air, but in the end, all the jugglers could keep three bags in the air at one time.

Ariel, a Cuban boy, played one of the giants the kids meet in a forest. In this scene, he had to walk on stilts. Other kids were birds and had to run and caw for the jungle scene. They raced across the room time and again, arms out, heads looking up and out and around, as if for danger. Some of the kids like Angie and Susana and Edgar had long speeches to memorize. Lines from the play were repeated over and over. "I like my friends because they have different opinions from mine." And, "If you want to finish the game, you have to find the light." And, "I was so nervous that my butterflies had butterflies in their stomachs."

After a long day of rehearsals, when their feet hurt and their voices ached, and they could not remember another dance step, the kids raced to the pool, where they cannonballed into the water and splashed until it was time to get ready for dinner.

Because of the many hours they spent rehearsing and working together, the kids were learning to understand each other even though they spoke different languages.

They learned to read each other's faces to see if what someone said was funny or sad. They were beginning to trust each other more and more.

My Music Is Different From Yours

The play needed music and songs to make it come alive. Cuban children grow up surrounded by salsa, a special music that combines the classical Cuban music called *danzon* with the beat and rhythms of African drum music. Because it is a mix of so many different things, the Cubans call it salsa, which is the Spanish word for sauce. Cubans think of their salsa as sauce with lots of spice.

Some musicians were invited to the camp to help the kids learn about each other's music. Amadito Valdez, a drummer with the world-famous Cuban group The Buena Vista Social Club, brought his drums and set them up in the sunny rehearsal room while everyone lay down to concentrate on the sounds. "These are timbales," he said, and the room throbbed with the shake and beat of the two small drums. Hollow metal objects called cowbells were attached to the stand holding the drums. Amadito played different rhythms, using the timbales and the cowbells. "This style of rhythm," he said, "came from the beat made when farmers ground coffee beans."

After he played, everyone was excited. Ray drummed a beat, and a circle of kids surrounded him, dancing and clapping.

The next night the rappers Afu-Ra from New York and Edgar Álvarez from Havana visited the camp. Afu-Ra was visiting Cuba for a hip-hop music festival. Edgar was in a Cuban hip-hop group. Then one by one, kids and mentors rapped stories about themselves in Spanish or in English.

Later, the musicians worked with groups of kids to write a rap song that would be in the play. Soon they were all singing "No Fear," the song they had written. *"Sometimes so much happiness is going on, sometimes we want to experience something else. . . . ,"* they wrote. No one called it a Cuban song, or an American song. It was just *their* song.

Old Havana

A day off! Angie and Evelin decided to explore Old Havana, settled about five hundred years ago. They invited Ray and Ariel to join them. After a long week of rehearsals, it felt wonderful to sit along the Malecon, the wide boulevard that borders the water in Havana, with nothing to do but enjoy the sun on their backs. Cuba's shoreline is rocky along the Malecon, but in other parts of Cuba, wide white sandy beaches stretch for miles.

When they walked into Old Havana, they saw a street theater group in the main square. Evelin told Angie the group was acting out a Cuban folktale about a blue unicorn. The actors

were on the highest stilts that Angie had ever seen. "I'll be as good on my stilts in our play," said Ariel, as they watched the actors dance and run on their stilts over the old cobblestones.

Three women walked by, dressed in costumes from the Spanish Colonial Period, when Spain ruled Cuba. Angie and Evelin borrowed their fans. They imagined what it must have been like to have lived and worked on a plantation long ago, with only a fan to cool them in the muggy humid heat of Cuban summers.

Ariel and Angie found a sidewalk gallery of paintings. One picture showed the old homes of Havana with new buildings rising behind them. The sky was yellow and the buildings were crooked. The artist had painted

what he felt, not what he actually saw.

Down the street from the paintings was a group of older musicians. They were retired and now played for tourists in Old Havana.

Music is the country's national pastime.

There is a saying in Cuba that if you turn over a rock, under it you will find a musician.

The kids found a shop selling *cabasas,* dried pear-shaped gourds. The gourds have grooves running down the length of them. When beads strung on a net are wrapped around the gourd, a scraping noise rings out, similar to when pebbles are shaken in a tin can. Ariel beat the air with maracas, gourds filled with dried peas, and Ray drummed on a set of bongos. They pretended they were a band playing salsa music.

26

Ariel put on a beret at a souvenir shop. He told Angie that it was a "Che" beret. Ernesto "Che" Guevara, a doctor from Argentina, was a hero to the Cuban people. Che fought beside Fidel Castro during the revolution and later died fighting to help poor people in Bolivia. Children say *Seremos como el Che* ("We will be like Che") in school every day. There are many posters of Che in Havana, always wearing his beret.

Visits Home

In the afternoon, Evelin and Ray wanted to show

Angie where they lived. They stopped at a line of taxis, most of them cars from the United States brought to Cuba before the revolution and embargo. Cubans have repaired their cars over and over for forty years, sometimes painting them the same color as their houses. Ray took a picture of his sister and their two friends.

Evelin and Ray live with their mother, a school counselor, and their father, a physical fitness instructor, in a suburb of Havana called Alamar, which means "by the sea." Built after the revolution to help with the housing shortage, Alamar is row after row of concrete apartment buildings, with gardens, playgrounds, and outdoor fruit and vegetable markets scattered in between them. It has a cultural center, too, where Ray takes painting classes, and where Ray and Evelin first started acting with La Colmenita.

Some of the apartments have been recently painted, but many have old paint that is peeling and baked pale by the sun. Flowers and potted plants hang off the balconies, and everyone keeps the stairways swept clean.

Sometimes neighbors get together to fix up their buildings, using materials bought at a

low price from the government. Other groups might ask the government for low-cost materials to build a new apartment building or house.

Evelin and Ray's dog raced down the stairs to greet the kids. The kids' mom had heard all about Angie, so she got a big hug along with Evelin.

Evelin's mother was making tamales for the children in the play. Evelin showed Angie her Barbie doll and Ray's stamp collection, filled with colorful stamps from all over the world. Angie also collected stamps. "I have this one, too," she said, pointing to one from Mexico. They looked at an atlas, tracing the shoreline of Cuba and

running a finger to Los Angeles. Evelin showed Angie places she had been in Cuba to visit relatives or for La Colmenita shows.

"I want to go to Spain with La Colmenita," she told Angie. "Maybe the next time they go, I'll get a part."

Angie pulled on a crocheted hat, and her short hair created a fringe around it. With a laugh, Evelin's mother gave it to her, telling her she would crochet another one for Evelin.

Evelin and Angie looked through a jewelry box in Evelin's mother's bedroom, trying on earrings and bracelets. Finally, they polished their nails and strolled into the room where Ray and Ariel were still playing Nintendo.

Before the kids left to go to Ariel's house, Evelin's mother served bread pudding, flavored with peanuts and coconut. This is a treat that she makes for special occasions such as Mother's Day, Father's Day, and Children's

Day, which is celebrated every year in Cuba on the third Sunday of July. For birthdays, Evelin's mom buys a big frosted cake and uses matches for candles, if candles are scarce. If Evelin

doesn't have a gift to give her mom or dad on their birthdays, she says, "I don't have anything to give you—just a kiss, my best present!"

Now it was Ariel's turn to show Angie his house. A neighbor who had a car drove the kids down a long gravel road close to the sea. Two cows grazed peacefully under a tree across the road where he lives with his mom, a pharmacist, his dad, a filmmaker, and his little brother. The house once belonged to his grand-parents, but when their children married, they moved down the road. Ariel's mom and her two brothers divided the house into three apartments, one for each family. Because of the housing shortage in Cuba, many families divide their homes.

Ariel told Angie that he had a surprise for her. He and his uncle were building a Japanese rock garden. They used big rocks to outline a large yin/yang symbol. Ariel had learned about this in his karate class. In the center, Ariel had a line of boulders, then rocks, then pebbles, which flowed like a river into sand. Ariel said this showed how the big

problems in life can become as small as a grain of sand if you learn how to make the best of things in spite of your problems.

Ariel's mom squeezed fresh mango juice, and his dad picked a coconut from a tree so everyone could drink the juice from inside the coconut. His grandparents walked down the road to meet his new friend. They found Angie and Ariel in the hammock on the large patio off the kitchen, reading one of Ariel's favorite books, *The Little Prince*. The grown-ups drank thick, sweet Cuban coffee.

The next day, Evelin invited Angie to her first day of school. She was in the sixth grade,

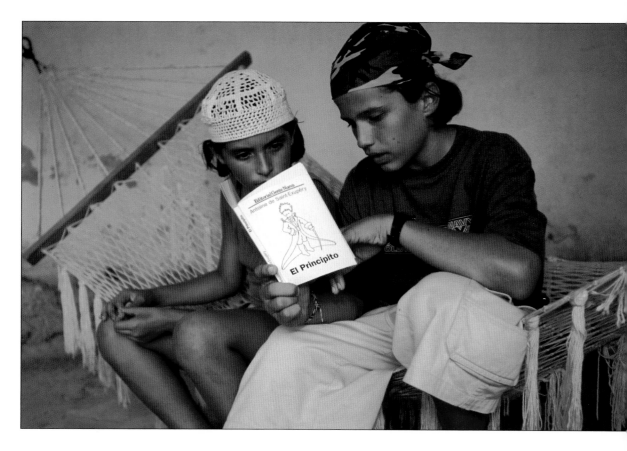

and this was the last year she would wear the red tie of the lower school. The kids were excited to be at school. Back-to-school carnivals in towns all over Cuba celebrated the beginning of school. Television spots reminded Cuban kids

to get their notebooks and pencils ready. Billboards around Havana showed children reading stacks of books. Mothers carried huge decorated cakes to school. Today was for fun. Tomorrow was soon enough to start classes in math, Spanish language, history, government, science, and natural sciences, like agriculture.

Angie and Evelin sat at a metal desk, with books and notebooks. It wasn't so different from her school, Angie thought, only there were no computers. Evelin showed Angie one of her favorite quotes. *"Vengo del Sol, y al Sol voy, Soy el Amor, soy el Verso."* ("I come from the Sun and to the Sun I go, I am Love, I am Poetry.") It was by José Martí, a Cuban writer and revolutionary who had lived more than a hundred years ago. He was a hero to the Cuban people because he fought and died for their freedom from Spain. His poems and writings still inspire Cubans. Then Angie looked at the walls, which were covered with murals of kids working in the fields. Evelin told her that most middle and upper students in Cuba spend a few weeks in the country helping plant or harvest crops. This was José Martí's idea, too, because he believed that work and study should be linked.

Cuban kids join the Pioneers, an organization started by the government to give students a chance to try things they might not have in school, such as baseball or mechanics or music, and also to learn about the socialist system of government. Evelin was elected the leader of the Camping and Exploration Club for her Pioneer school group. Because of this, she is one of the students who can make decisions about the school, similar to the student council members in Angie's school.

The Countdown

For four weeks Angie had been learning lines and dance steps, hanging out, talking, and trading clothes with her new friends. She fell into the rhythm of each day—breakfast, rehearsal, lunch, free time, rehearsal, dinner, more rehearsal. Getting E-mail from home or hanging newly washed clothes on the line were fun ways to break up the day.

Angie had known that this month would be a lot of hard work. What she hadn't known was how much it would mean to her. "My friends all have a special way of showing love," Angie wrote for the play. "They are all different from each other. I like my friends *because* of this." She learned that people can be different but still be friends, because friendship can be based on working hard together.

It was hard for Angie to believe that they would all be on the stage of the National

Theater of Cuba soon, performing their play in a real theater in front of two thousand people.

Show Time

When the day arrived, it seemed as if everything was going wrong. The final dress rehearsal was here. The elaborate costumes made by the Cuban mothers needed last-minute safety pins, stitches, tape, or wire. Ray's feather necklace for his bird costume fell off each time he practiced his leap. Edgar toppled from his stilts. Angie and Evelin sat for what seemed like hours waiting for the mentors to help them with their makeup. Herenia, a Cuban doctor who had a child in the group, helped with makeup, too, outlining eyes in

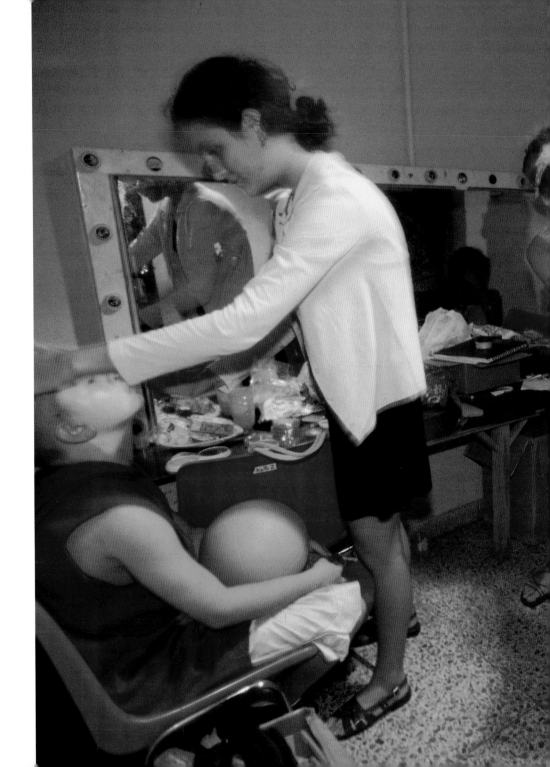

dark pencil and painting lips bright colors.

Lights—where were they? Jaime, the Cuban director, sprang into action, flipping switches, adjusting the sound system, moving part of a stage set to make it even more dramatic. Michael, the American director, stayed close to the stage, taking the kids through final instructions on where to stand and how to wear a microphone. He shouted "OK!" to Jaime when everyone was in place. If anything did go wrong, if someone forgot a line or missed a step or lost a necklace or hat, they knew to keep going with the line, the dance, the leap—with whatever it took for the show to go on.

Maybe it was really going to work after all!

After the rehearsal, Michael called for a break, but some of the kids continued practicing. Angie took this time to sit in the plush red seats in the theater and look with wonder on the show the kids from both countries had created. Ariel was on stilts. Angie thought about how he knew her favorite parts of *The Little Prince*. Ray was playing a bird in this scene. He flapped his long arms and made cawing noises. Angie thought about the many bird and animal stamps he had collected. Ivette, from Cuba, was wearing Angie's shirt. They had laughed when trying on each other's clothes the night before.

Reaching for the Sun

Outside the theater, brothers and sisters squeezed to the front of the line of parents. Most of the Cuban parents were coming to the performance. Even some from Los Angeles had traveled more

than 2,000 miles to Havana to see the show. Everyone was dressed in their best clothing.

The lights went down. The theater went black. Then the curtain rose, the spotlights beamed down on the actors.

There was Eraisy from Cuba, dancing with Corey from Los Angeles. Now Edgar came out and stood in a spotlight and recited his monologue without missing a word. Then Susana stood on the opposite side of the stage and said the same lines in Spanish. During the baseball game scene, it was hard to tell which kids were from Los Angeles and which were Cuban. They rapped and strutted and sang their way across the big stage. They had become one group, not the group from the United States *and* the group from Cuba. They *were* the SOL Project.

The audience gave them a standing ovation. They knew something special had happened during this month, both on and off

the stage. They knew that Cuba would be different, because of the kids, and the kids would be different because of Cuba.

When the big paper sun rose over the stage at the end of the play, the kids were supposed to reach their hands up toward it, as if to touch it. But instead of reaching for the sun, they reached for each other, and touched each other's hands. Then, grabbing tight, together they took their final bows.

Outside the theater, Angie took a deep breath. "This is Cuba," she thought. She felt she was leaving part of her soul in Cuba to mix with everyone else's soul. "Some things come from

your head and some things from your heart," she thought, "and now I know Cuba both ways."

Much more than the play had happened during that month. Although the play was over in one afternoon, the journey Angie had taken with her friends, old and new, would last forever.

Index